PIANO · VOCAL · GUITAR

Disney
FROZEN II

MUSIC FROM THE MOTION PICTURE SOUNDTRACK

ISBN 978-1-5400-8308-1

HAL•LEONARD®

Visit Hal Leonard Online at .
www.halleonard.com

Contact us:
Hal Leonard
7777 West Bluemound Road
Milwaukee, WI 53213
Email: info@halleonard.com

In Europe, contact:
Hal Leonard Europe Limited
42 Wigmore Street
Marylebone, London, W1U 2RN
Email: info@halleonardeurope.com

In Australia, contact:
Hal Leonard Australia Pty. Ltd.
4 Lentara Court
Cheltenham, Victoria, 3192 Australia
Email: info@halleonard.com.au

Contents

ALL IS FOUND

Music and Lyrics by KRISTEN ANDERSON-LOPEZ
and ROBERT LOPEZ

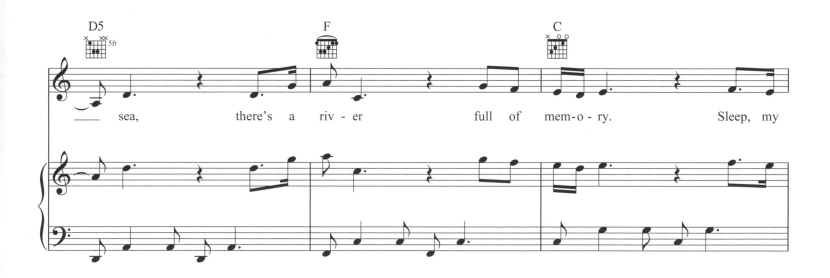

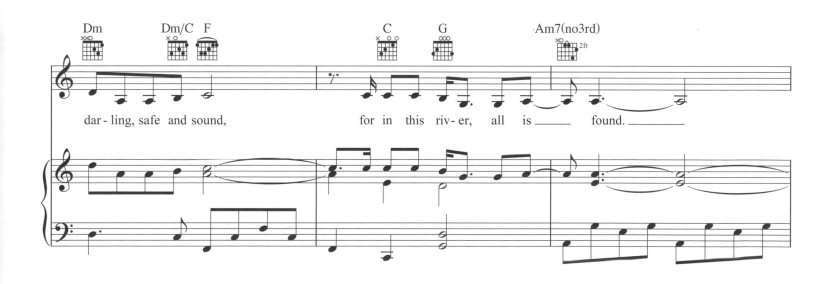

In her wa - ters _____ deep and _____ true lie the an - swers, and a

path for you. Dive down deep in - to her sound, but not too far, or you'll be _____

_____ drowned. _____ Yes, she will sing to those who _

_____ hear; _____ and in her song, _____ all mag - ic flows. _____ But

SOME THINGS NEVER CHANGE

Music and Lyrics by KRISTEN ANDERSON-LOPEZ
and ROBERT LOPEZ

REINDEER(S) ARE BETTER
THAN PEOPLE (CONT.)

Music and Lyrics by KRISTEN ANDERSON-LOPEZ
and ROBERT LOPEZ

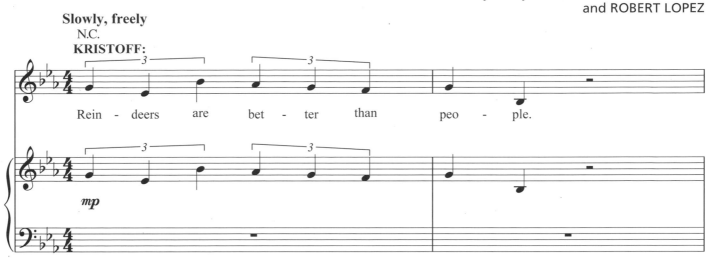

Slowly, freely

KRISTOFF: Rein - deers are bet - ter than peo - ple.

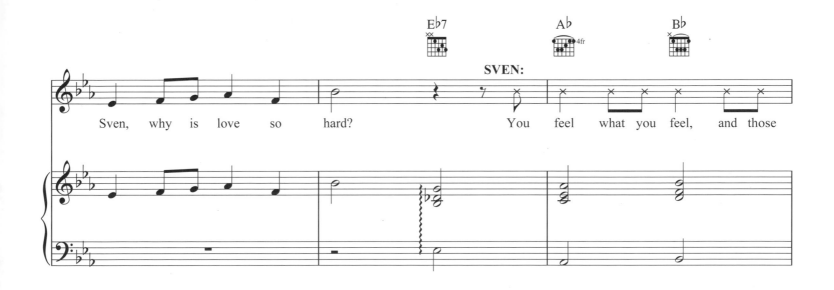

Sven, why is love so hard?

SVEN: You feel what you feel, and those

feel - ings are real. Come on, Kris - toff, let down your guard.

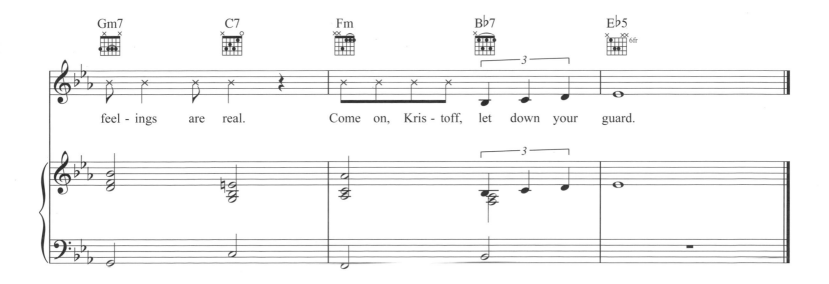

INTO THE UNKNOWN

Music and Lyrics by KRISTEN ANDERSON-LOPEZ
and ROBERT LOPEZ

WHEN I AM OLDER

Music and Lyrics by KRISTEN ANDERSON-LOPEZ
and ROBERT LOPEZ

OLAF: *What was that?!*   *Samantha?*

This will all make sense when I am old - er.

Some-day, I will see that this makes sense.   One day, — when I'm old and wise, —

LOST IN THE WOODS

Music and Lyrics by KRISTEN ANDERSON-LOPEZ
and ROBERT LOPEZ

KRISTOFF: A-gain you're gone, off on a dif-f'rent path than mine. I'm left be-hind, won-der-ing if I should fol-

40

SHOW YOURSELF

Music and Lyrics by KRISTEN ANDERSON-LOPEZ
and ROBERT LOPEZ

Ah, _____ ah. _____ **YOUNG IDUNA:** Ah, _____ ah, _____ **ELSA:** I've

nev - er felt so cer - tain. All my life I've been torn. _____

But I'm here for a rea - son: could it be the rea - son I ___ was born? ___

I have al - ways been ___ so dif - f'rent. Nor - mal rules did not ___ ap - ply. ___

THE NEXT RIGHT THING

Music and Lyrics by KRISTEN ANDERSON-LOPEZ
and ROBERT LOPEZ

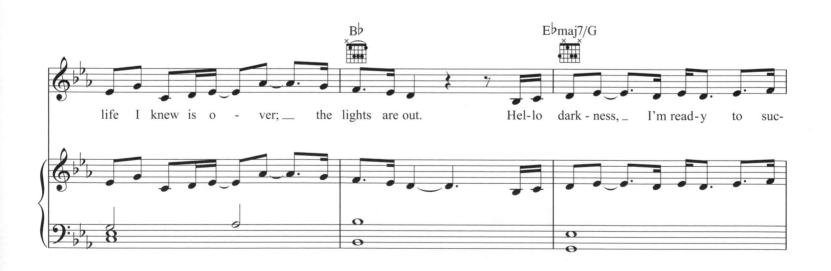